In

Out

3

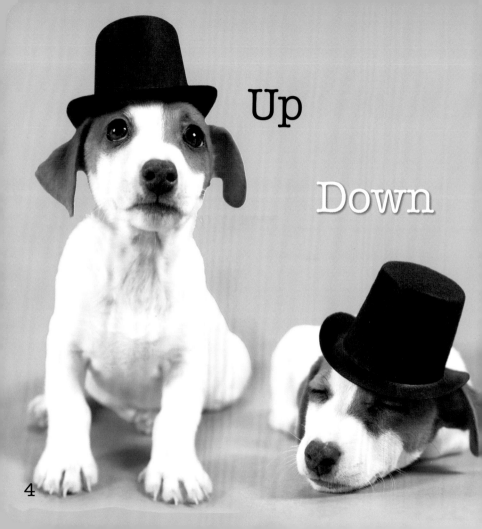

Up

Down

4

Empty

Full

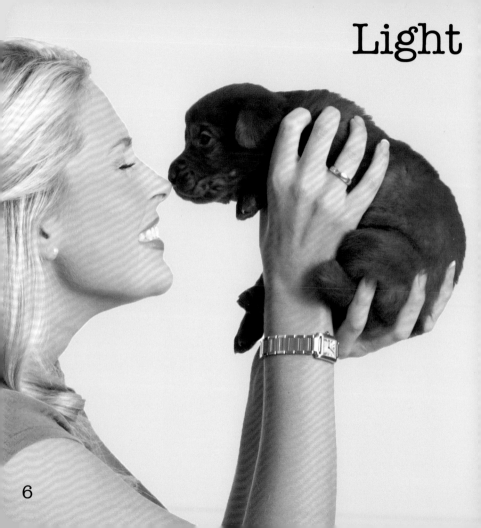

Light

Heavy

Happy

Sad

8

Long

Short

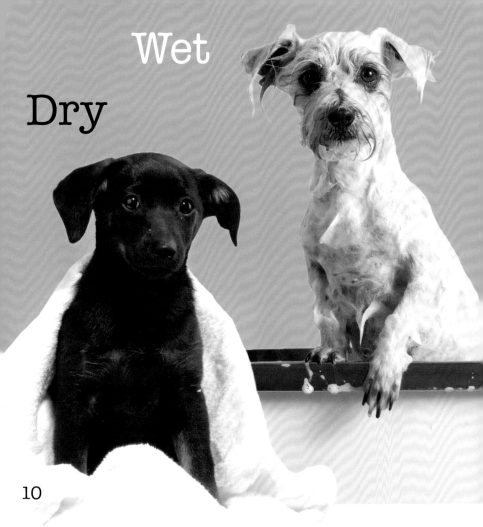

Wet

Dry

10

Fast

Slow

11

Sit

Stand

12

Big

Small

Asleep

Awake

Front

Back

15

The single most important way to help your children succeed in school is to read to them every single day.

Even before children can speak, books can help them learn sounds, shapes, colors, and the names of things.

Koochiching County Public Health
Follow Along Program
1000 5ᵗʰ Street
Int'l Falls, MN 56649

NOODLE SOUP™
OF WEINGART DESIGN

By Cydney Weingart

4614 Prospect Ave., Suite 328
Cleveland, Ohio 44103

(216) 881-0083 • NoodleSoup.com
Reprinted 05/17 • Product #9864

ISBN 978-0-9885075-3-1